running with a with a snow leopard

Pamela Beasant

Published by Two Ravens Press Ltd
Green Willow Croft
Rhiroy
Lochbroom
Ullapool
Ross-shire IV23 2SF

www.tworavenspress.com

The right of Pamela Beasant to be identified as author of this work has been asserted by her in accordance with the Copyright, Designs and Patent Act, 1988.
© Pamela Beasant, 2008.

ISBN: 978-1-906120-14-6

British Library Cataloguing in Publication Data. A CIP record for this book can be obtained from the British Library.

All rights reserved. No part of this publication may be reproduced, stored in a retrieval system, or transmitted in any other form or by any means, electronic, mechanical, photocopying, recording or otherwise without the prior written permission of the publishers. This book may not be lent, hired out, resold or otherwise disposed of by way of trade in any form of binding or cover other than that in which it is published, without the prior consent of the publishers.

Designed and typeset in Sabon by Two Ravens Press.
Cover design by Iain Ashman.

Printed on Forest Stewardship Council-accredited paper by Biddles Ltd., King's Lynn, Norfolk.

About the Author

Pamela Beasant, originally from Glasgow, now lives and works in Stromness, Orkney. She has been published widely as a poet and has written many books for children. In 2006, her play, *A Hamnavoe Man*, was performed at the St Magnus Festival. Her biographical study of Orcadian artist Stanley Cursiter was published in 2007 by the Orkney Museum, and she is working on the final edit of her first novel and a libretto for an opera in collaboration with composer Gemma McGregor. In January 2007, Pamela was appointed as the first George Mackay Brown Writing Fellow. *Running With a Snow Leopard* is her first full-length collection of poetry.

Acknowledgements

Poems from this collection have previously appeared in the following places: *Chapman* 55-6 and 86; *Casting a Spell* (ed. Angela Huth, Orchard Books); *New Writing Scotland* 13 (eds. A.L. Kennedy & James McGonigal); *Northlight* 1 and 2; *Northwords* 22 and 28 (featured poet); *Cold Kye, Curlew Cry* (Soulisquoy Printmakers); *Norman MacCaig, a celebration* (ed. Joy Hendry, Chapman); Wordworks exhibition (Highland Printmakers); *After the Watergaw* (ed. Robert Davidson, Scottish Cultural Press); *Daffodil Time* (ed. Anne Thomson, Galdragon Press); *There's a Poem to be Made* (ed. Christine De Luca & Ian McDonough, Shore Poets, Edinburgh); *Riptide* (eds. Sharon Blackie & David Knowles, Two Ravens Press).

Special thanks to Penny Fielding, Stewart Conn, Joy Hendry, David Knowles, Sharon Blackie, Yvonne Gray; and last and first, to Iain, Alex and Tom Ashman.

Grateful acknowledgement to the George Mackay Brown Writing Fellowship, 2007, for the opportunity to work on this collection; and to the Scottish Arts Council for a writers' bursary in 1999/2000.

Foreword

I write this foreword with a sense of at least a little bewildered incredulity. This woman claims not to write about landscape, but she does, superbly well. Speaking of Orkney, where she lives, she says: "the sense of being a pinprick, on the edge of the world, is accentuated here. It's frightening, or comforting, depending on the mood." Pam, you're right about being a pinprick, a pinprick on the all-too-thick skin of this world. You, and we, must realise just how potent that prick of a pin is.

I've seen this before: women who, while chronologically 'no longer young', are reborn, aged maybe forty-plus, who suddenly come into their own, almost debilitatingly self-conscious – modest, literally, to a fault. Pam Beasant *does* write about landscape, especially Orkney but also elsewhere, in such palpable terms that you can feel the particular light of the curious conversation she so eloquently describes between sea and sky, sea and land, sea, sky and land (because all are quite different) in such a way that you feel you are there. She writes about her husband, her children, her own feelings with intrinsic purity – and, more importantly, simple craft, so that we see into her life as a mirror of our own. We feel it poignantly as she experiences it, and can take it into our own lives, with whatever sense counts, loss, fulfilment, regret... Whatever the reader might bring to listening into her life, we are welcomed into it. A childless woman myself, she allows me to share in and enjoy the joy in her children. That is rare indeed. And all this is presented on a gentle plate, not at all threatening, or presumptuous. More than that, it is all set against a background of a vividly described, timeless land and sea-scape which, whatever our circumstances, we can all step into.

Pam's poems bring together so many things. This is a woman 'coming into her own' – and there's more to be had from her pen than yet dreamt of – especially, I suspect, by her. She offers up to us a perfumed chalice of integrated experience – integrated almost magically in a way I bet she doesn't understand yet, and perhaps never should. Deliberately echoing Rilke's celebration of the act of saying: "Are we here, perhaps, for saying: house,/ bridge, fountain, gate, jug, fruit-tree, window –/ at most: column, tower ... but for saying, realise,/ oh, for a saying such as the things themselves would never/ have profoundly said.

So, 'word', 'sea', 'sky', 'land', – and just *saying* these is miraculous in itself, and Pam makes these words reverberate *tellingly* in their varied contexts and uses. Of all the many poetry books and manuscripts I have read in quite a long career, this one stands out as 'the start of something big'. It is a start: there will be much more, as Beasant learns confidence in the voice she patently has already. She makes no apology to fashion, literary trends – the refreshing thing is that she hardly computes them (save in her nice riposte in 'The writer's deadly sins' to Faber et al). Her point is that these poets do *not* prick her skin – she pricks her own, and ever so gently, letting our sensibilities, consciences and imaginations out to play on the gentle thoughts and images she gives to us. And, most potently, she gives us the quiet space to prick life for ourselves, or massage our own space, if we wish, or are ready to do so.

This is a poet of so many landscapes, geographical, human, emotional, all brought together with what can only be described as febrile sensitivity, understanding and forebearing in a way which is totally non-careerist. In every word she writes, she is there, in a totally non-eogcentric way, and enabling us to put all aside in an act of communion with whatever we might individually decide is greater than we are, be it a writer like Norman MacCaig, George Mackay Brown, the 'great unknown' – or whatever. This book lets us join in; we are welcome parrots on her shoulder, never excluded by her, or stimulated to do so by our selves, as I find in much new writing. There is no 'me, me, me' here. She abandons herself to her subjects with star-like humility and a profound and unselfconscious acceptance of their character and essence. Surprisingly perhaps, there is real drama in some of these poems, especially 'In Orcadia', as she unfolds the unwonted tragedy of David – one of the finest poems here – which could easily become a play.

In this collection, Pam Beasant runs with far more than snow leopards: she manages to run with every subject she touches on – and these are varied – from motherhood, to 'literary matters', nature, and the disabled women she worked with, celebrated so powerfully here. She pays homage to her poetic inspirations – MacCaig, Brown, Stewart Conn, Yeats – I detect Louis MacNeice and others too, evoking both their personal spirit, and their work with perhaps just a little too much deference. She needs to step into her own role as poet, and relate herself to others from that position. We are left with a deep sense that in the end, there is only all of us, looking at land-, sea- and sky-scape, our society and ourselves, joining hands in a search for the truth.

In writing this, I fervently hope that she will never lose this innocent insouciance and powerful unselfconsciousness, which is liberating, although even the act of saying *could* destroy it. But I don't think it will.

Joy Hendry
Edinburgh, 2007

Introduction

For me, poetry has always been an instinctive and internalised occupation – a secret place. From being a child, I have always written poetry, and this collection was written over several years. There are many themes and prompts for poems, but they all come from a strong emotion, or from a moment that is significant in some way; and they are mostly to do with people – or the self in relation to others. Some are an attempt to come to terms with major upheavals. My father died when I was eight; an event that obviously changed the world and left me looking for a person I can barely remember, or exploring the gap left. Others look for meaning through the idea of god (which I've always wanted to accept but never could), or literary heroes such as Yeats and Norman MacCaig. Some are domestic, about the children. Others were inspired by a stint as a part-time care worker, doing everything for four profoundly disabled women. This was a revelatory experience. I'm not sure if I had much impact on them, but they certainly did on me. Orkney is a prompt, too, though I don't often write about landscape. But the sense of being a pinprick on the edge of the world is accentuated here. It's frightening, or comforting, depending on the mood.

Pamela Beasant
Orkney 2007

Contents

Part One

The touch of a hand	3
Yesnaby	4
View from the garden	5
Tumbling cliff	6
Tourists	7
Phenomenon	8
In Orcadia	9
Out with my loves on a windy day	10
Tom's arrival	12
Running with a snow leopard	13
On pregnancy	14
You two	15
One man band	16
Feeding Tom	17
Finding you in Rackwick	18
The calm	19
Weighing hearts	20
Parted by the Atlantic	21
Haunted	22
History	24
The anniversary	25
Ten lines of greeting and goodbye	26
The blackening	27
Volcano	28
Had enough	29
The old man	30
Before the birth	31
Billions	32
The approach	33
Yasha	34

Part Two

Autistic tendencies	39
Curry for breakfast	40
Trying to read Angela	41
Jean, depressed	42

Part Three

The writer's Deadly Sins	47
God discovers modern art	49
Numbskull	50
How long does it take to write a poem?	51
Memorial refrain, for T.W.N.B.	52
St Magnus Day, 1996	53
Farewell to Stromness	54
Letter to George	55
Meeting the composer	56
Iconoclasm	57
Iris Murdoch, with Alzheimers	58
Visions of William Blake	59
Beyond words	60
Betrayal	61
Guilt	62
Stenness Loch	64
Finding Mallory	65
Fishing	67
Land/mind	68
Writing in public	69

*Dedicated to
Brenda Blakeley*

Part One

The touch of a hand

There are no images for God
only ravaged stillness
like a river-bed where rocks and plants
incline the way the water used to flow
over their dryness; they look as if
they still believe it covers them.

Hand in hand we walk where the river is not
and the moon ghosts limbs cresting
the flowing mosses, compelling the eyes
up, to the gap in the night.

Yesnaby

The cliffs are caught
in a stone tremble,
a slanting moment of change.
The sea, volatile pedant,
lashes and caresses
its argument into the land's
resistance.

The bitten
apple with a bruised core
decays in the flash
of a thousand years.

View from the garden

The hills have no secrets.
At dawn they stretch their colours out,
unfold to the gradual levels of the light.
As evening declines they gather coherence
to a menacing silhouette.

At midnight I sit and concentrate
the darkness of my mind on the hills;
it is echoed and dispersed,
thin through soft air; it doesn't resist
the thrust of a gull's wing.

A sudden boat
glides a slow domination across the scene
leaving a soft sea spine; ribbed clouds
reflect in the water, their rain-bones
trail to dust on the fleshy swell.

Voices, pleasant, neighbourly,
almost visible, clack like ping-pong balls
across the earth's table. Cheerful words,
not probing too deep, incise the calm,
interrupt the pulse from the hills and the sea.

Tumbling cliff

The cliff falls head-first
into the sea. It lies asleep,
not dead, for seaweed
sprouts on its head, and the sea
combs it with the care of a child.

Tourists

In a northern summer, at pale midnight,
running from the green and powerful sea,
we scramble to the slippery, craggy places
and watch with the dead lovers of the islands.

We see nothing, we don't move,
enclosed under a wide, wide, sky;
it is more happiness than we want,
more peace than we know what to do with.

Taking the memory of busy places, we lay it
in bare earth and wait for judgement;
but there is nothing, no symbols or pictures,
we dig it up again and draw it back inside ourselves.

Uneasy – we feel that the mountains
are harsh and the sea has cruel purposes
for our white bodies – we feel
the cliffs crumbling underfoot.

But when darkness comes, the sea
doesn't sleep, and when our eyes
open to morning, it doesn't wake,
and it restores us.

Phenomenon

The cliffs are ripe and ready
to fall, forming barriers
against the tide and the sun
on the lapped shingle below.

We are there at the moment they fall.
Great slabs slide endlessly
silent onto hard wet salt
and the dry bay where they push
down and never move again.

A rabbit and a sea-bird,
stunned in the descent,
land with one thud in gentle rubble.
Fur and feathers
stiffen, mould together
into a strange breed of death.

In Orcadia

There's a luxury in watching the sea;
its liquid muscle flexes in the tide. Mass force
grumbles warnings, which nobody heeds.

Sun on the water catches David's eye
and he looks away, annoyed,
thinking about the harvest coming in,
and the worry of it all,
and the dull pain left by the death of his mother,

and the sharp pain when he sees his father
with some other woman.
Someone shouts his name – he squints,
sees the peedie boy from up by,
eyes sparkling, come to ride the tractor.

Out of habitual kindness he welcomes the boy,
digs up tatties for the family
(whose crop had blight this year).
Two days later his father found David,
shot through the head, lying quiet in his room.

Today, there's a big turn-out for the funeral.
The small boy frowns,
puzzles intensely over the mystery.
David said he could ride the tractor Sunday,
He didn't say he planned to be dead by then.

A new, sharp-bright stone goes up;
it has the luxury of watching,
forever, the flexing sea.

Out with my loves on a windy day

We walked anti-clockwise round the shore path,
defiant, straight through the steel bars of the facing wind;
the hills of Hoy stood near and remote
strips of strong light fanning their dark sides.

My loves and I were walking in the wind
on the very rim of the world.

The rubbled path tickled Alex's feet
and she teetered on sturdy shoes.
She laughed as her hair streamed out,
kicked through her zigzag of interesting wrack;
wondered where the (storm-blown) sand had gone,
felt my coat pocket for polo mints.

Iain, half in and out of his thoughts,
collected firewood, found something for Alex,
ambled bear-like, watchfully, this way and that.
And the Ola, wind-caught, shot past Ness Point
in a dogged, lurching mainland dash.

I felt the familiar ferry pang,
Left behind, although I don't really want to go.

We battled through the campsite,
up the South End, past the cannon, red-limbed,
out of breath, till the gale broke
on hard, historical stone.

We had come widdershins to Stromness,
but the town was gracious, it let us pass;
we finished our walk, my loves and I,
came home on a windy day.

Tom's arrival

I broke apart and you came
in the rush and twist, fist first, of your birth;
face folded up against the rasp of air.
And my breast loomed larger than your head.

My midwinter boy.
We lay in our storm abatement.
The rain pounded the roof,
and you slept.

Running with a snow leopard

Eye to eye through the wire fence,
no surface in the long, connecting silence.
Your arm moves a fraction,
the leopard flicks his tail.

Suddenly you run the fence's length
like a young wind. He follows,
full throttle, veering closer,
mirroring the ecstasy.

He crouches ready to spring.
You copy. Both
brimful of dangerous joy
prepare to meet.

The fence looks low.
Reaching out, fearful,
I capture you back,
to the lesser, leopard-less world.

You match a lithe pace to mine,
nature reinstated;
but in your glance back at the animal,
I catch naked collusion.

On pregnancy

I would not be udder-breasted,
bloated like the drowned,
floating on the edges of myself
in watery dreams of birth.
I would not be in back and womb-racking
waves of pain for a half-dead day
to force a sticky blue conception
of a thing, half-you, half-me,
of bones and water, skin and brain.

You two

Blue swimsuits, white legs; reflections
shimmering and darting in the paddling pool.
You two, my loves, my hopes,
sitting in the same small space.

I have quite forgotten
life beyond you.

The long, bright, childhood tunnel
encloses us all.

One man band

Scotland the Brave booms out
again, your mouth a large
O of serious noise. Hands
bang the biscuit tin with

beautiful timing as strong
knees pump up and down
with military poise.
(Good kilt knees, we say;

you nod, complacently.)
In your head the full band
sweeps across the room
weaving here, there

and back again in wonderful
convolutions. You follow,
chock-full of glory
and music, head held high.

Feeding Tom

Breast and cheek; two roundnesses
moving together for milk, for comfort.
Eyes concentrate, fingers search my face.
Some part of the connecting brain
lies adrift inside a soft skull.

In diagrams, the nipple's sucked right down the baby's
 throat;
Sketchy drops of milk don't show the cannon force of it;
the hunger. It's a miracle you don't choke.
You choke. Recovering, you find the food again,
pulling on it urgently.

Expert at this rigmarole, you fill
and slow and sleep. A tremor
moves across your mouth
like an omen, as reluctantly
you let the nipple go.

Finding you in Rackwick

In Rackwick bay, stones are pink
with the effort of smoothing so much time
into perfectly flawed roundness.

They lie in a colony,
a petrified spawn of dinosaurs' eggs.
And from this distance the cliffs are tame,

postcard pretty. A fulmar
wheels from its nest,
tilts the world away from the sun.

A distant speck
jumps through the binoculars,
detaches from the steep and slatted rock,

becomes a little figure, running;
a tiny chaos making for an open shore.

The calm

Sleep, tiny girl,
while the sea,
sea-green, cold,
lovely green,
sucks at the teeth
of the town.

You are far
from storm wind
and hail sting.
Little voyager
sail back safely
from your dream.

Weighing hearts

Judgement day, today.
You sit, masked,
ceremonially robed.
Plastic scales adorned with stuck-on hieroglyphics.

Trembling, I kneel.
You take my heart
(a blob of pink plasticine),
weigh it against a feather.

Down goes the heart.
Slowly, you take my hand,
lead me to the underworld
(a duvet over the sofa).

At the last moment, mercy.
You stick some lego in beside the feather.
Saved, on appeal. You smile benignly,
pulp up my pink heart without a second thought.

Parted by the Atlantic

You sit by the ocean
I sit by the sea.
Walk in. You'll find
there's no need to breathe.
Walk on the sea-bed
at the base of the undersea
mountains. Walk
round them.
I'll sit here
until your head emerges
seal-like, watching
from your ocean, my sea.

Haunted

It's been an elastic time since the death;
compressed, then stretched to oblivion.
A lifetime is like that, your life
must have seemed like that to you.

Now forced through ink on the page, you are
used wantonly. A man, clever,
methodical, you liked silly songs,
and died before I knew who started me,

or realised who was gone.
Sometimes I try to die the death
you faced; but can't rehearse
the long, black thing,

or free you to it, shadow puppet
dancing in an artificial light.
If I stood courageously, and still,
would you emerge with substance,

colour? Would you take me
utterly, or let me go?
I wish you wanted to test me,
that you were my green knight, that involved.

I stumble at death's thin coat tails,
it doesn't turn; for me the blank eyes
will not reveal and burn. My hand
closes on nothing, to a fist.

A face darts and lingers like
a trick of the light; sometimes hard,
strong and bright. A glance
crumbles it in a green flash.

History

From Glasgow to Cornwall every year
I studied the back of his neck as he drove.
At Calderpark Zoo, invariably, I said –
Are we nearly there? And the neck would
redden a little.

It's not much to carry from a life,
but when my son, with great seriousness,
bends over toys,
his neck looks just the same,

which provokes a startling rush
of grief and fear.

The anniversary
for Sylvia

His death formed in her gut like a stone;
an obstruction she learned to by-pass
putting off the operation.

Its rough, heavy presence blocked all paths
to him, made no demands except to
let it lie there. The day came when she

reached in, unplugged her own gut, held his
death, extracted, in her living hands.
Grief, like arterial flow, glutted

the breach, unstemmed. No comfort; except
the part of him inside that patches
her will stay, grafted on the tissue

to make it heal, and the stone, shut tight
in a drawer will be accessible,
benign; all the sharp surfaces smoothed

by her intricate imprint.

Ten lines of greeting and goodbye

Blood drains from your forming shape;
dying, you bob in the one soft place
you want to occupy in the world.
No harsh light, hard surfaces for you,
banging out your heart and soul
against life's drums and bricks.
Slowly you let your hold slip,
slide out dead through the birthing place,
over the brink of your long, black space;
weaned before your captive mouth can suck.

The blackening

Drums and clatter in the back of the pick-up,
young men shouting, drunk, emboldened,
faces streaked with tar and spit.

The boy whose wedding is announced
by the ragged, peacock display
sits mute, uneager, filthy.

The women watch from the cafe.
– Is it John getting married? – Aye,
it's no witty all that drink and racket –
– And cauld. Rather them than me.

Left cling-filmed to the Market cross
he catches the last light oddly in his modern stocks.

Volcano

My angel,
violence-maker,
hot harbinger of death.

A black arrow pierced me.
I hated you for this forcing up,
this heaving of the world.

After you left
I lay dormant, looking for you,
for an erupting love.

Your frail hands never touched me.
My memory does not record a touch.
I run my fingers down a cold, wax arm.

Yours and mine.

Had enough

The leaden comb
holds in its teeth
a few more silver strands of hair.
She's a featherweight on life,
a flimsy, ancient map
preserved in a museum
all pink and flannelette.
the last relic of a hopeful country
long since struck by drought.

The old man

So roaring, so reared by the wind
whipping up in his face, the smile
a black crack of pleasure and
doom for the stupid, the teeth
stalwarts of storm and erosion,
the eyes a shock of life, half-shut
in the lair of the droughted cheeks.

Before the birth

Do not spill me,
I am as fragile as ripe fruit
in a gust of wind.
Truth is the opposite of truth
and feeling of feeling.
That's why I know
I am happy
when tears fall around a dry stone.

Words are not strong,
another is always more perfect
another way of putting things
is better. Peel back the sound.

Everything moves,
torn about by the tearing quiet.
Shadows forget where they were before,
the spilling is effortless.

Billions

Billions of people dead;
billions of up-turned faces
horizontal in an earth bed;
billions of tons of ashes,
fuel spent to counteract
the lack of space,
and we're no nearer to the mystery
of empty carcasses and lack of breath.

The approach

Drawn into time,
gradually you come.
With weather-beaten wings,
the desire to make honey
you toss and dither.
Hunting us out.

Does the Earth hang
by a thread? From where you are
only you know,
or may see it in this way,
spinning in a dangerous arc
as you approach.

Closing in,
you move darkness around time's force,
spy the danger suddenly,
prepare your sting.

Yasha

Queues filed, naked, children quiet,

Yasha was in demand at parties,
his eyes danced and his hair curled
in a way the other children loved.
He was touched by magic (they said),
usually won the games.

babies hidden in bundles of clothes,

Yasha stood beside his mother,
stroking the head of his baby brother.
His father was strong.
Finding them.

found, thrown in anyway.

Yasha filed into the room for a shower,
looked for all the places
where the water would spurt out.
His mother held him urgently,
he shook her off impatiently.
The baby found her naked breast
and drank as the gas poured in.

Darkness racing in their minds,

Yasha died in shock,
was bull-dozed into a pit
spread-eagled over an elderly baker
and a dull boy from his home town.
His mother and brother were several layers away.
As the earth went in,
it filled the cracks between heads and limbs,
covering them;
neatly covering them all.

death undoing so many.

Part Two

Inspired by working for four years with profoundly disabled women, who taught me that the world isn't altogether as it appears.

Autistic tendencies

With a finger pressed on an eye,
the room obediently tilts;
shadows jump, colours frazzle,
bleed an inch then spill in all directions.

Sounds roar, one from every colour,
panic wells from your diaphragm;
a sudden hand soothes your back,
moves in, as if from far away,

a voice says all right, it's all right,
and it goes, the terror, the room slides back,
interestingly, the way it looked before
when you were here, long ago,

or was it minutes? Are you the last one
waiting for the aftermath of shadows,
colours, sounds? Thin fingers reaching out
to test an alien world.

Curry for breakfast

Today there is fierce debate among your carers.
You were given curry for breakfast.

You saw orange and yellow kaleidoscope in the bowl.
They saw dignity drowning in pilau rice.

You tasted sweet and sharp and hot.
They feared gossip and disapproval.

You speared, expertly, a pepper,
let the light refract through glistening onion.

They put cereal back on tomorrow's menu.

Trying to read Angela

Like an illuminated manuscript
with unfathomable text
you come alive in margins.
Life consists of them;
the main subject passes you by.

I wish I could appreciate
the detailed pattern and depth;
this art of the periphery.

A genius of silence,
interpreter of multi-layered space,
you are brave in this lonely place,
reaching out, occasionally,
reading the full text of somebody's eyes
for a second – for a curiosity.

A break from the frenetic work
of weaving invisible sense from colour and shape
to colour and shape,
across a terrible word abyss.

Jean, depressed

I look like a stick insect somebody stood on;
long, cadaverous face
frames wide, pale eyes,
reflecting all of me, concentratedly,
all the hopeless effort to work in any other way.

Don't be moved by this,
because, by God, I mean to frighten you
for all your gracefulness, all you assume.
Cold hands lift me in the morning
deftly from shower, to bed, to chair,

prodding pressure marks
where bones stick out; applying
deodorant, lotion, powder, cream,
and fresh clothes every day.
Then a sudden soft brush on my hair.

Meal-times are a kind of hell;
food feels like matchsticks going down
sideways; stopping dead half-way.
You are kind, but I can't understand
this grindingly constant care.

If I were free,
I wouldn't spend all this time
with me. I'd put a pillow
over my face
if my hands would work that way.

I wouldn't give a painful shit
for any one of the last, long, fifty years.

Part Three

The writer's Deadly Sins

Envy/covetousness

They're elegantly kerned and leaded,
the Faber books;
too lovely to read,
almost.
They're objects,
the poems,
artefacts,
epitomizing typeset taste.

We're Faber poems
they say,
you'll have to get past
the look of us first.
Even then,
we might not speak
to *you*.

Anger/envy

Bastard.
Who the fuckity-doodle-doo
d'you think you are?
Strutting about –
you have to work quite hard to be so
cock-sure casual.

*I'll just read my latest concrete poem –
can you see at the back there?
It's in the shape of a wee cloud.
This is specially for my editor,
it's her favourite.*

Bloody hell.
I thought concrete poems went out
with the bloody ark.
I'll make a concrete poem of you, son,
feet first, in a foundation stone.
The grave of the unknown poet
buried in a block of flats
(a wee cloud sits on top).
There's poetic justice,
ya bas.

Sloth

There's something there –
the way she looked,
eyes naked, then masked.
He winked before he left,
hard or oblivious.
I could write it down –
those moments that speak, well,
not volumes exactly,
but a pithy wee poem,
a character piece.

I *could.*

God discovers modern art
(for Howard Hodgkin)

Suspended here above delicious green,
the asthmatic rasp of pink,
hard blue swirls around a tiny square of plaster white,
so delicate,
you could break it up
looking too long.

Deep colour penetrates the general malaise;
red and gold
fringes my splashing birth.
More fun this
than all the Masters with madonna
and cloying, sumptuous child.

Diving at you,
scaring you out of your wits,
I'll feel for a moment
speed, eye, flesh, air, lung, breath, skin.
Blink, I'm off again.
You won't believe your atheistic eyes.

Numbskull
(for Norman MacCaig)

I visited you years ago;
heart in my mouth,
shaped into my best, heart-shaped smile,

leaped off the train at Waverley,
gazing round expectantly.
You walked home from Haymarket,
probably fuming.

We met, eventually,
you might not remember.
I, another numbskull in the long parade of them
through your life. But I won't forget your
x-ray eyes,
kindness,
breath-stopping poetry.

How long does it take to write a poem?

MacCaig, wily old master,
trotted out the unvarying reply:
two fags.

It always drew a laugh.

He meant
don't over or underplay the art.
Don't make it god.

But his eyes –
Suilven pools smarting in a Rose St pub –
betrayed the devotion of a life spent
watching, smoking,
filling volumes.

Memorial refrain, for T.W.N.B.
(After Memorial, *by Norman MacCaig)*

I am your sad music;
I die everywhere we go,
I die slowly just as you bob up again.

You dive like a sea-bird
I jump like a fish.
Passing each other
we curve out of our elements.

Look, my hand can shake and twist,
it can clasp another's,
it can almost touch the mountain of your image
lurking in my mind.

I can kill you off in any sunrise,
by un-thought, in any city square.
I am free,
I am free to die like you.

St Magnus Day, 1996
(for George Mackay Brown)

Shadow on the stone
echoes the angular jut of your chin;
fleetingly, you are everywhere,
except in the box being lowered down

and it's hard to leave you there,
to not look after you, bring blankets
for the cold, and soup to nourish, to show
that you had made it to another spring.

Old men weave a spell of death,
tangle in it willingly,
drop from the end of a history
that tries to breathe, and can't.

This will be the day we start to repeat
by heart the litany of a book slammed shut.

God and Magnus, Island, Hamnavoe,
squandered a feast of images through
one life; took you, feather-light,
left us circling the gap.

Exposed on ancient contours,
pinioned by an inexorable sky,
we stand on this St Magnus day
at Warbeth, silent, where you lie.

Farewell to Stromness
(Peter Maxwell Davies played this piece at George Mackay Brown's funeral on St Magnus Day, April 16, 1996, in St Magnus Cathedral.)

Fingers push out
the catch and thrust,
the simple repeat;
tension,
building to anger, desolation,
for the death of the poet,
and Stromness without him;
for the mouth-stopped islands
the gap in the world.

Loss distils into lilting harshness.
Notes pour out;
a torrent of hail on the heart.

Letter to George
(i.m. George Mackay Brown, 1921-1996)

The last of the September light
is all but gone, the equinox past too.
Birds are shrill in the trees.
The moody weather-splendour of October settles in.

How your heart would sink at it –
the prospect of winter stretching out –
only St Lucy, with her steady candle,
holding at the heart a little flame.

From the magician's trick of heaven, do you
see Hamnavoe, as if from high above? Or,
are you wrapped around us omnipresently;
twinkling, without blue eyes to smile from?

Impossible, we are Stromness again,
though different now; not earls and tinkers,
fishermen with ploughs. And all things
will pass like you; like time; will flash and die.

Meeting the composer

Lizard-like, he darts about
then sits stock still.
The obsessive eyes don't seem to blink.

The mouth is deftness in reserve,
it exudes a fierce, defensive
music intelligence creeping in
through some undeveloped sense.

There are words there, measured,
carefully framed. They don't translate
the intense mercurial score of him.
A halting libretto cannot be made to fit.

Iconoclasm

Lenin; massive, face down,
trundled off to a retirement park
to stand beside himself and Stalins
(and the KGB man with all the zzzs),
in a strange, still parliament of clones.

The people jeer euphorically.
I understand why, but am sorry
for the smashed-up eyes,
the broken dream.

And the mob,
though probably right,
is ugly.

Iris Murdoch, with Alzheimers

A body moves from room to room,
parting space randomly.
Like something abused, it shrinks
from the world, creeps somewhere safe
if anyone intrudes, confuses the air.

No longer meeting herself, she ekes out days
of unquiet, swimming in fog,
aware, moth-like, she must get somewhere –
the light – and death the blind by-product.
Peaceful when asleep, alone in the sea,

the numbing sea, where life is not a compromise,
but altogether a new philosophy.
Self snagged under her own sprawling net;
thrown back indifferently –
the twitch of a dream.

Visions of William Blake

Hard words swirl and blind about your head
like hail on the angels and patriarchs.
Imagination crams your space with people holding forth,
looking stunning, forming Miltonic son-et-lumière
at a never-ending private show.

Poor Blake, the crack-pot, existing
reed thin, sweat-drenched in a dream;
virtual reality, ahead of your time;
ill from being a jobbing prophet all your life;
unhonoured, the way it always seems to be.

Sweet revenge now when you materialise
with wings, white robes,
paraphernalia, mocking our sleep,
penetrating a struggling, empty space; telling us,
after all, the gods have never really changed.

Beyond words
(for WB Yeats)

How I dislike your gyres and towers and lustings
for the arrogant Maud Gonne – old man fantasies
banging on. And yet, not quite remembering
who they were, I cry for Leda raped
and Agamemnon dead; your nine and fifty swans all
flown away, and as for that ridiculous
Byzantine sea, torn by dolphins, tormented by gongs –
I understand the longing and the intensity.
Layers of meaning, despite the vocabulary,
live still through myth and artificiality –
twist in the deep, revolving wonder of your poetry.

Betrayal

What's the core of a life? Is it
to think you are something,
or have something? Or is it not
to know – to find it
with new coordinates each time?

The view from a window; the way
light plays on the land,
or the way you see it, can change;
life's map gone awry,
monsters outlined among the gaps.

How can love lie – what does its true
taint look like? Is it visible
– like outlines? What does
its removal leave behind?

Love, a trammelled, mire-sodden thing,
can gather in a
ball of dirt; be hurled in one
brutal parting hurt.
Betrayal, worse than a clean wound

can maim or kill; or set you free
on a strange map – stark, brave and new.

Guilt

Full of happiness I sit and watch
the tide confuse itself on slabs of rock
and sky, sea, hill and bird
set out a world of perfect order.

I think of you when darkness comes
wakeful in the city-yellow night,
body ghostly-white in pictures
of the past, mind reflecting turmoil.

We spoke before I left; I admired
how the conciliatory sound
fell in patterns on the distance
put between us, glad to be alone.

But on a calm day, when the light falls
pink on ancient stone, polishes
the wood of door and window-frame
in the grey cottage, you are the seal
edging closer carefully,
in the bay that is swept with sparks
from the sun of the dying day.

In a thin note, high and drawn,
it sings about an approaching storm,
and soft eyes blinking in its barrier face
have a look of you that stretches out
shadows of the peace.

I watch the seal accusing me
of treachery and forcing out
the image of your face across
this land that will not shelter me,
yet sees nothing, tells nothing, thinks nothing.

Stenness Loch
A postcard to Stewart Conn on his seventieth birthday

S eals take to the water at the Brig O'Waithe; sudden elegance as stiff
T ails become expert rudders, bodies sleek in their
E lement, they play in stolen light of the late summer day.
W ish you were here to find words for that
A dept display. Further round the loch, near the watchstone,
R ipples from a small boat, a ghost-silhouette of an angler, line
T aut, expectant, as he lingers in the bay. At

C ock crow, for you, a seal song merges with a northerly
O ver the Firth, Grampians, Pentlands, joining a
N ew sound - a celebration from all the airts -
N ot just for what has been, but an underwater treasure
    to be reeled in.

Finding Mallory
(The body of the climber, George Mallory, lost on Everest in 1924, was found by a team of climbers in 1999.)

Everything safer now –
our metaphorical Everests, with corpses tidied away.
The climbers who found you (scientifically
kitted out), were unprepared for this alone –

your body mummified blinding white
to a death-cast, casually lying there.
Unpecked, the muscles showed in outline
beneath the waxy skin. Remnants of torn clothes

clung redundant to bone-flesh; nine layers,
amounting to less than an inch, of cotton and thin wool.
Head down, the body thrust, arms curved and raised,
like a swimmer doing a crazy frozen butterfly.

Announcing your fall and cause of death, one leg bone
stuck out, cracked, while the foot, intact,
still lay inside its hob-nailed boot. A scrap of woollen
    sock
flapped like an insistent ragged flag.

They found an altimeter (broken), letters,
an unpaid bill, goggles in your pocket (no spares),
a boyish nametape on your shirt.
Identity proclaimed,

they found a horror in the lack of face
a patient haunting in you, waiting
all this non-time, for the last
loneliest moment to be scrutinised and shared.

The wild mountain never cared, and the question
prompting the search, of whether or not you reached the
    top,
is unresolved. Rock-moulded, your body
forgot the importance of it, how you pushed and broke it,
    years ago.

And though they covered you with stones –
tidied the corpse away – they took you home with them,
flesh recorded, their souls bare.
They took you, dead and clinging, into all our Everests.

Fishing

I can't write you out,
form an edge with words,
pull you from my body.
Instead, I sit with a hook in my brain
trying to catch a bit as you flash past.

Sometimes I reel in
a smile; the shape of a hand; pipesmoke.

Land/mind

Landscape, satisfying word,
hard-edged, mobile, varied, green.
Mindscape is silvered, dangerous,
too vast and fleeting. Milton's hell
exhaling from a mouth long dead.

Patterns extracted from the land,
hay stacks, fence posts, standing stones,
thread the air;
mind mosaics are mist-edged,
time hissing through gaps.

Writing in public

A face on a stick
in a spotlight;

leavings of someone else
in a chipped desk drawer
wiped clean.

My turn now.

Books with loose, comforting
library wrap, stand on the reserve stacks;
yesterday's papers, folded in pigeon holes
line the wall.
They seem to politely wait.

Darkness falls.
Through curtainless windows
I'm glowing out to the town's abyss.
Sit. Write.
Push ink over
the rope bridge of the page.

Poetry from Two Ravens Press

Castings: by Mandy Haggith
£8.99. ISBN 978-1-906120-01-6. Published February 2007

Leaving the Nest: by Dorothy Baird
£8.99. ISBN 978-1-906120-06-1. Published July 2007

The Zig Zag Woman: by Maggie Sawkins
£8.99. ISBN 978-1-906120-08-5. Published September 2007

In a Room Darkened: by Kevin Williamson
£8.99. ISBN 978-1-906120-07-8. Published October 2007

In the Hanging Valley: by Yvonne Gray
£8.99. ISBN 978-1-906120-19-1. Published March 2008

The Atlantic Forest: by George Gunn
£8.99. ISBN 978-1-906120-26-9. Published April 2008

Butterfly Bones: by Larry Butler
£8.99. ISBN 978-1-906120-24-5. Published May 2008

For more information on these and other titles, and for extracts and author interviews, see our website.

Titles are available direct from the publisher at
www.tworavenspress.com
or from any good bookshop.